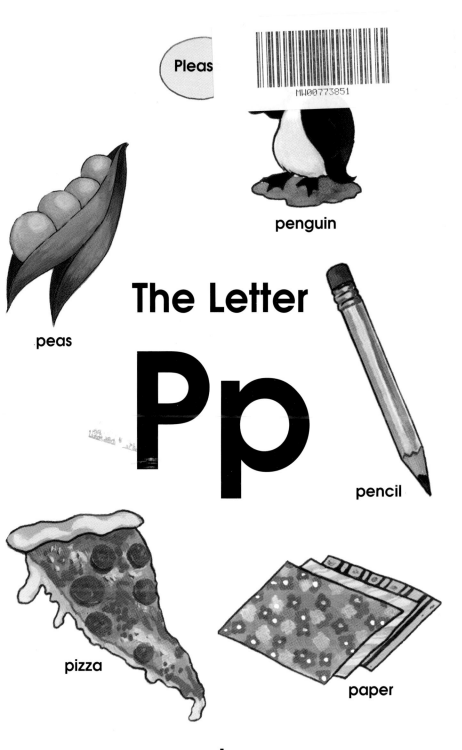

penguin

peas

The Letter

Pp

pencil

pizza

paper

1

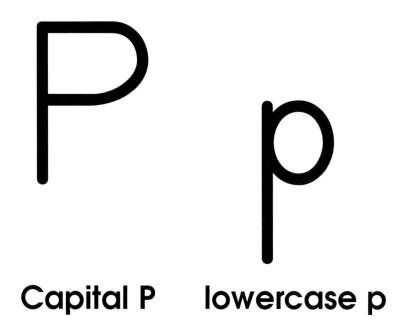

Capital P   **lowercase p**

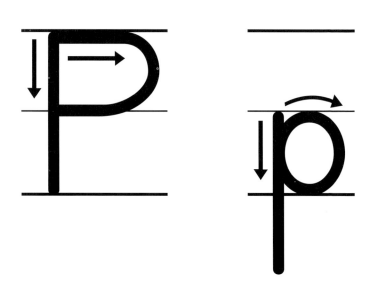

This is the way to write Pp.

**Pp is for
penguins playing.**

3

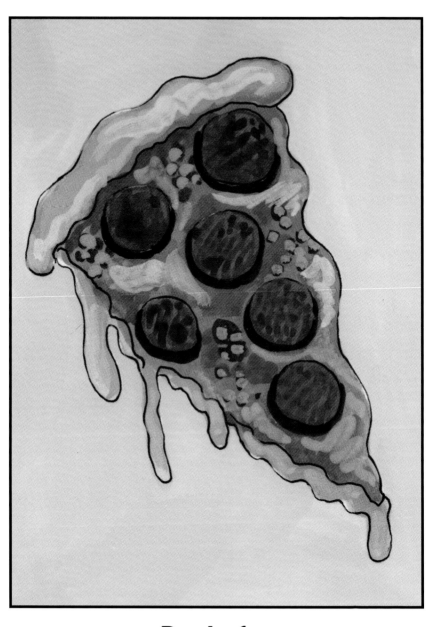

**Pp is for
a piece of pepperoni pizza.**

**Pp is for
peas in a pod.**

Pp is for
pretty paper.

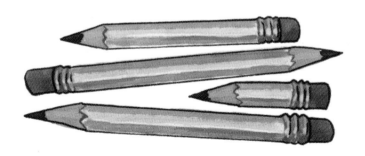

Pp is for
pointed pencils.

Pp is for
polite words like
"please."

Pp is for penguins,
Pizza and peas,
Paper and pencils,
And polite words
like "please."